LYNN RUSSO

THE STEPS OF MY
LIFE

Poetry for the 12 Steps

authorHOUSE®

AuthorHouse™
1663 Liberty Drive
Bloomington, IN 47403
www.authorhouse.com
Phone: 1 (800) 839-8640

Published by AuthorHouse 10/12/2016

ISBN: 978-1-5246-1109-5 (sc)
ISBN: 978-1-5246-1108-8 (e)

Library of Congress Control Number: 2016908630

Print information available on the last page.

Any people depicted in stock imagery provided by Thinkstock are models, and such images are being used for illustrative purposes only. Certain stock imagery © Thinkstock.

This book is printed on acid-free paper.

Because of the dynamic nature of the Internet, any web addresses or links contained in this book may have changed since publication and may no longer be valid. The views expressed in this work are solely those of the author and do not necessarily reflect the views of the publisher, and the publisher hereby disclaims any responsibility for them.

Tribute

Lynn Russo,
mother of three,
faithful friend to many,
died on January 10, 2014,
one day before her 65th birthday
and just a short while before
this book was published.

For those who knew her personally,
we know we were blessed.

For those just getting
to know her through her poetry
you are equally blessed!

May her words touch you
in the way you need to be touched,
Amen.

Lynn's Dedication

I would like to dedicate this book
to my English Professor,
Ivan Goldfarb, without whose constant
accolades of my essays,
I would never have taken up the gauntlet to create this
inspirational work for all the still
sick and suffering alcoholics.

My lack of self-esteem would have prevented me
from taking, "The Road Not Taken" (Robert Frost).

TABLE OF CONTENTS

A Friend of Bill W. 1

Birth Of A Foster Child....................................... 3

Betrayal 6

Frustration.. 8

Divorce- 9

The Journey.. 10

Igneous Imagery.. 12

Independents Fear 13

Heart Attack 14

Full Completeness.. 17

Illusion 18

Step 1 21

Newcomer 23

Eves' Skirt 24

Wounds that Bind.. 26

Ego Deflated.. 28

Touch a Friend 30

Step 2 33

Have an 'L' of a Day... 34

Anonymous 35

Through today and tomorrow 36

Nightmare 38

Step 3 39

Out of focus.. 41

In Decision... 42

A Tired Minds' – Plight.. 43

A Work of Art- Our Father who Art in heaven.............. 44

Step 4 47

As Grace Beckons 49

Clean your closet 50

Put Gratitude in Your Attitude.. 52

Step 5 55

Eyes Wide-Shut 57

Fool's Gold 58

Step 6 61

Rebellion is Fatal.. 62

Step 7 65

Lord I Am Not Worthy 67

Step 8 69

A Quiet Objective View... 70

Prayer of True Repentance 71

Step 9 73

Serenity 75

Step 10... 77

Patience and Persistence 78

Step 11... 81

Waiting for the Snow to Fall... 82

If I Knew Then?.. 83

Step 12 85

As Winter Wanes.. 86

Soul food 88

The Ocean Liner.. 89

The Fishers On The Break 91

The Phoenix.. 92

The Greatest Commandment 93

The Flower and the Breeze 94

Denise 96

10 Year Testimony Of Sobriety And

In Praise Of A Sponsor.. 97

Lynn's Unfinished Autobiography 99

Know That I Love You 103

From Here To Eternity 105

A FRIEND OF BILL W.

Much like the tribal shamans who painted their faces as a sign of power and wisdom, life had painted crow's feet upon Kurt's otherwise unblemished face. There was an angular crookedness to his jaw, matched only by his owl-like beak. His pearled flesh had the spiritual aura of a glazed icon. It was an aura that traveled upward across the territory used in the placement of a hand for a blessing. A few wispy hairs marked this territory – once graced by a full compliment. Like arrows, the tiny crow's feet attracted attention to his rather deep-set, earth-tone eyes. Most times they seemed to radiate with inner peace and flowing serenity but, often, they overflowed into pools of sadness created by the curvature of mans' destruction of self. He would leave this world as he had entered it, toothless, but for now, loose fitting dentures grated across his gums. A hearing aid nestled in wiry tufts of gray-white fuzz.

His strength came not from a muscular physique. A birth deformity had turned his spine into a question mark. Slightly hunched and in the twilight of his years, he was also prone to attacks of emphysema. But, his nobility is statuesque and he stands as tall as Gulliver in the land of the Lilliputians. "What did she say?" His hearing impairment forces him to struggle desperately to catch the works of others. He turns his head, straining his neck. His hands are cupped behind his ears. His brow in furrowed ripples resembles a freshly plowed field waiting the planting of new crops. Yet, more often than not, silent syllables are all that fall within his grasp. He sighs, trying to force air into his damaged lungs. He speaks in short breaths but, words slide across his tongue like hot, melted butter.

His is the story of a dramatically, devastating childhood, the degradation of deformity and the downward spiral of self-worth. The consanguinity of this heritage left him with an affinity for consuming alcohol in excess. This seemed to be the only relief from his overwhelming pain of body, mind and soul. Hence, in his early twenties as he describes it, "I was a broken man." He speaks carefully and slowly in a Mark Twain rhetoric. "The pursuit of my illusions brought me to the gutter. The guilt. The shame… I had become the man I most hated-my own father. I was so sick I knew nothing, but fear. I weighed less than one hundred pounds", he continued. "And I was powerless." Powerless! Those words echoed in my head. Had I not written a poem, "Powerless To Heal?" His power was his ability to meet a not-so-perfect stranger and make them feel like family. He was truly a friend in need…in deed…Indeed!

BIRTH OF A FOSTER CHILD

My child is not a babe
That grows within my womb.
My child is anothers'
Born of whom?

Beyond my soul,
A power to believe.
No swelling in my breasts;
And yet, I conceive

Aborted, all alone
The family womb ejected
Away from the heart,
Self-preservation protected.

And then, that breath
Of total air
Where germs may be present;
But, someone can care.

I'll hold you, my child;
And, help you to grow.
It will be painful;
And, a little slow.

Together we'll learn
Of things we can't change;
But, we'll also learn
To rearrange.

I too, someday,
Must let you go;
But, not 'til you're ready
And, you will know.

When the time is right,
And, you are you.;
And, not a child
Who wonders who?

Who am I?
Where do I belong?
When does the sun shine?
What is a song?

And, in my heart,
Your life will be
Not of the womb;
But a part of me.

Betrayal

Pushed beyond the strength I had; I found I could survive.
I jumped the mountains precipice; And still, I stayed alive.
Beyond most human endurance, I dared to take a chance
I had to know the truth; If perhaps, for just a glance

It saddened all my being; And, really wrecked my brain.
I thought I'd never sleep to dream; or, dream to live again.
I know now, I can bear it. But, I should want to kill.
And, on an angels wing, I sleep upon a hill.
My eyes are burning fires, Smoldering in the rain.
My heart is oh so saddened. I have never known such pain.

I feel, as though, I'm beaten. The fates have dealt a blow.
I know that I will find a way. But, I feel so low, low, low.

I wish that I could sail away, for just a little while.
And, dream that all had ne'er occurred I really need to smile.
But, the box has just been opened; And, the snakes are all
around.
Slithering and hissing. I cannot stand the sound.

Would that I were deaf and blind. Facts are hard to face.
Bad dreams are all I see tonight. Thoughts-I can't erase.
It makes no sense to me, at all I feel not wrath nor fury.
I cannot do the sentencing Nor, be the judge or jury.

I crave some freedom from my thoughts; And peace, my heart be brave
It does no good to ponder ill; Or I shall start to rave.

I'm tired now, for all is done. It almost did me in.
But, I will not surrender Howe'er, I cannot win.
I'll walk the earth in emptiness. A puzzled look on me-
For, what was once by God so blessed; Is now God-damned to be!

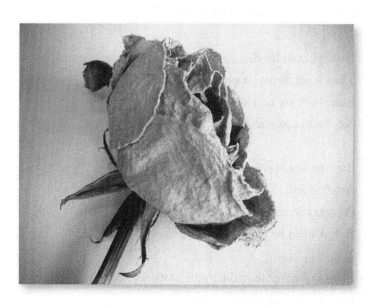

FRUSTRATION

Buy me a flower.
Anyone will do
A pretty fresh flower
But, it must be from you

I toil and labor to pull all the weeds.
In my little garden I've planted new seeds.

I can't understand it. Why don't they grow?
I want pretty flowers all in a row.

I'm trying so hard.
They have plenty of sun.
But, there are no flowers.
No. Not even one

Buy me a flower.
Anyone will do
A pretty fresh flower
But, it must be from you.

Plenty of water to make them grow tall
But, no, not one flower-none in all.

DIVORCE-

Death In Valor Of Reborn Central Essence

Tears are hidden in her gaze,
Melted snows of ice cold rage.
Slipping over razors edge
Of baked enamel, to the hedge
Sliding off the branch that lives
To the rock- that never gives
Painting wet- the rock, half-in
Streams a trail, that's never been.

Along the trail- a beaten path
With hearths of stone, and hearts of wrath
Upside the hearth, willows wave
As if to mark a site- so grave.

Yet, up the hill- from trials trail
A seedling sits- that will prevail.
Prevail as winds that show the way
Blowing in- the answers May.

THE JOURNEY

Once upon a lifelong journey, she stops to look and has a yearning. Yes, so dimly she remembers the Decembers dying ember in the hearth of loves dismember

Then she bolted and emoted. Pitter, patter on the floor. T'was her tears and nothing more. For, only she was jilted and her fragrance slowly wilted from the love that was before and never more.

>   And, the whistling corduroy- swished and swished with audible
>   sobbing in her chambers' bed. She bled. Pitter, patter – tears of red.
>   Fears unfledged..

With a slow emergence and the strength of true resurgence
>   Enters woman –virgin to a world of drunken bitterness.
>   Drink and purge
and years of ten to splurge and regurge but she cannot emerge.

Igneous Imagery

Conjure a candle-shimmering in smoke
The glimmering glow of light lazily leaping across opaque
orbs.

Mark the movement-overshadowing the obelisk
The flickering flame of light prismatically providing eluding
embodiment.

Entomb the ebony-damming the darkness.
The optimal optics of light fearlessly firing hyper optic
haloed hope.

INDEPENDENTS FEAR

Flowing red
No child in my bed
Only me −a child in my head
Sterilize my dread.

Cutting white
Incisors out of sight
Tigers tooth uprooting at plight
Vanquish my fright.

Turning blue
Your foot is in my shoe
They are mine. Mine to wear I grew.
There's no room for you.

Heart Attack

I've suffered-
    Pulmonary arrest
Involving complications
    Of arterial sclerosis.

Blood is seeping
Through the cracks
In the cardio vascular
Edema.

My lips are dry and blue.
My tongue is swelling.
Paddles---
    Stand clear.

Inspire,
    Expire,
Inspire,
    Expire,

As my labored breathing
Racks my chest,
Heaving heavy sighs,
I gasp.

Clouded visions-
My Children's tears
Weight my soul.

I cannot escape;
The gravity-
Of the situation.

I'd cry,
But, there are no tears;
Just an overwhelming feeling
Of being;

Of being swallowed up
And drowned.
Inspire,
      Expire,
Inspire,
      Expire.

My eyes
Are heavy with sadness.
And from beyond my vision,
Familiar faces call- with clear voices;

Undaunted,
By the shallow air.
Spirits,
Pure spirits- 100 proof

Inspire,
Expire,
Inspire,
Expire.

Surgery-
A by pass
Even pure oxygen-encased
Becomes a pillow.
Villainizing my visage.

I'm in an airtight vault,
On a throne
Of feathered pillows.
They allergize my bronchi

Inspire,
Expire,
Inspire,
Expire.

I did not think!
I could die twice?

Full Completeness

Inspired by the bible – Job 28:23-3 & 28

My soul treads in places forgotten by the foot of man. Seeking life's worth. To find wisdom and dwell in understanding; but, it is beyond the price for rubies and it cannot be bought with pure gold.

I dance in delight to the puppetry of Gods loving fingers. They are truly digits that confound the mathematicians and scientists.

Rockets may soar and roses bloom while, in between, we find the room to slither and slink with deceitful disdain. And align our course with the devils domain.

ILLUSION

I've drawn an illusion,
A feast fit for the blind.
No paper is needed,
Just presence of mind.

What else would I use?
But, Invisible ink
For what I have written
Is all that I think.

Now, this original copy
Is one of a kind.
The only dimension–
The perimeters of the mind.

And, I don't need a desk
For with a quick gust
My illusion is gone
Like skywriters' dust.

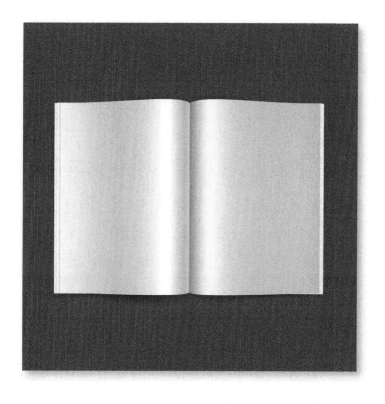

Step 1

*We admitted we were powerless
over our addiction - that our lives
had become unmanageable*

NEWCOMER

Newcomer, my little angel
You have come back to see.
Fly no more as stranger
But, rest on wing-ed tree.

Your face will bloom a smile.
Your eyes will simply rest.
Away from good and evil.
The tree of life to test.

The thunder of the cymbals
Will hum a lullaby.
And a clap of lightening
Will twinkle in your eye.

EVES' SKIRT

A fig for the figure,
As waves lap the shore.
What a price —for an apple core?
(Cover the whore.)

Now, to skirt the issue,
How do I feel?
"I need a heel!"
(Adds sex appeal.)

Like the shade of a lamp,
It must fit the stem.
"Raise up the hem!"
(Ah, what a gem!)

With a lemons' appeal,
If chosen in haste,
Lumpy as wallpaper paste.
("Where's my taste?")

But, over it all,
"I strut like a pheasant!"
Wrapped like a present.
("Isn't it pleasant?)

To turn the skirted dressing table.
This cover for shame,
Which was meant to tame,
(Just adds mystery to blame.)

WOUNDS THAT BIND

Powerless to heal
The wounds that bind
Man of many,
Yet, one of a kind

A broken heart can scar
And mend.
But, a casted heart
Can never lend.

"Do not touch the hurt-
You feel."
More than this,
You cannot deal.

An open wound
That always bleeds.
An oozing ulcer
That always feeds.

Unbind your wound
And give it light.
Look at it closely-
Then put it out of sight

Look to your heart
To heal what ails.
A tender touch
That never fails.

EGO DEFLATED

I drank with neglect of others around. But, now with respect, we humbly bow I see the challenge; A mountain at best. Step one we bow and give it a test.

A power so strong, we can feel the force If we just listen, He shows us the course. A loving arm that means us no harm,

but, guides us away from John Barleycorn. With compulsion lifted we can make a choice. For now we have an ego deflated inner voice.

TOUCH A FRIEND

I called you, and you answered.

I only had to dial.
It's like you know.
I need to hear words to make me smile.

If you just even listen;
and, let me tell it all.
You can even disagree;
But, I just had to call.

And,

somehow
through the fates
God has joined us each
to be there for each other.
within each other's' reach.

Step 2

Came to believe that a Power greater than ourselves could restore us to sanity

Have an 'L' of a Day

Like a baby you cry for stuff.
No delivery and God is just a bluff.
Rely don't defy.
Your Higher Power is a super guy.
Open your mind to a path of faith.
Gods' will for you is full of grace.
Have an "L" of a day
Look, Listen and Learn to pray.
Listen to others; look at you and your vanity.
Learn to get honest and see the insanity.

ANONYMOUS

"Hi! I'm Margarita and I am an alcoholic. First, I would like to thank the speaker for taking the meeting. Secondly, since this is my home group, I would like to share that I have been going for tests all week. I have agonizing pains in my lower abdomen and quite frankly I'm scared."

"The doctors have me on antibiotics but have not yet discovered the cause. Tomorrow night they should know if I need to go into the hospital. Thanks, for letting me share."

It's been almost six months since her last drink. She knows drinking is not an option. The compulsion of the addiction would only destroy any hope for a life of peace and joy as promised in the "Big Book" Of Alcoholics Anonymous. She knows drinking is just a slow emotional and spiritual death before the physical demise. No! She has learned enough to follow the suggestions of those who have gone before her.

THROUGH TODAY
AND TOMORROW

As mourning mist weaves its' magic spell, Melting structured steel into a mirage.

Enhancing, I do not wish to tame or change Just to intertwine dancing.

And, as dewdrops are fused into the suns' beam Radiating dispersed light into an arc

Coloring each day while nights gallop into the sunset Castle bound in honor.

Awaiting, is the promise of your tomorrow If you desire- today.

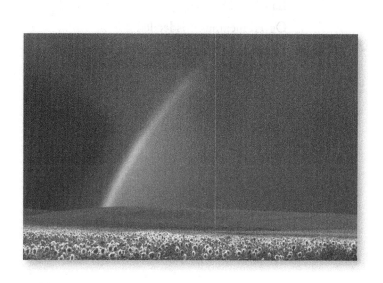

NIGHTMARE

As quickening quiet
Quelled my deep
Slumbering demons
Un-slumbered my sleep
Bated and beaded
Ogred meanies misdeeded
I galloped –though still in the crypt.

Step 3

Made a decision to turn our will and our lives over to the care of God as we understood God

OUT OF FOCUS

What is out of focus
When all we see- is the faults of others?
I, my, me.

What is feeling,
When all we touch-is rock, paper, scissors?
And who makes the cut.

What is tasteful
When buds don't bloom-not salt or sugar?
I am-I presume.

What is aroma?
A dead flower has no bouquet
But, the blossom it once was
Is a memory pressed away.

What is it I hear
When words are spoken?
Are they words of pleasure
Or is all silence broken.

What is the sense
To all of our senses?
If there is no response
and no kinetics.

IN DECISION

Half a head I fall to rise.
Stepping in I close my
eyes. Looking up I
say a prayer Not
to win…but,
just to fair.
Sigh a
sigh; for dare I dare.
All's up in
smoke—if I don't care.

A Tired Minds' – Plight

Soulful eyes
Haunt the skull,
While gray ghosts loom,
In the limelight of life's' longevity

While cobwebbed gray-matter,
Devilishly paints pictures of distortion
Old tired lines
Tease taut tissue.

Haunted- undaunted
Through the gray fog,
Omnipotent
Are the shadows

A WORK OF ART-
OUR FATHER WHO
ART IN HEAVEN

Must not the bow find grate across the string;
For much intended music to the ear.
If not the violin a song to sing:
Why play the instrument for all to hear?

No statues shrine be seen in hardened rough;
If hollowed without sculptors' pow of hand.
A raspy file to feel and rag to buff;
Hammer to chip; coarse grade to sand.

Hunger the artist with his souls' sweet guile
From whitened canvas or a paper sheet
With mighty brush in hand to stroke a smile
Once blank, for all to see a lovely treat.

Not only, irons' heat can burn and scorch
But in time, wrinkle free hangs the cloth.

With loving gratitude to my creator, my God

Step 4

*Made a searching and fearless
moral inventory of ourselves.*

As Grace Beckons

As grace beckons,
the mergers silently quaked.
For conscious and soul cannot be slaked.
Reunions rumble apices the dreams.
While contemplating silent screams.
The fissure bereft both spirit and mind,
While crevice cracked on course aligned.
But, grace was fathomed from the deep,
by foxhole prayers and anguished sleep.
Welcomes all who visit in trial of gut,
born of injustice or whatever the rut.

CLEAN YOUR CLOSET

Put your feelings on the shelf
Clean the closet – find yourself
Keep the good and
Trash the rest
Do per the sponsor
With whom you are blessed.

More than just a pretty face,
God has blessed you with his grace
Now take a step to share your glory,
With God and friend and self- don't worry.

Put Gratitude in
Your Attitude

Although our minds are blinded with tears of remorse,
May our hearts be overjoyed with the presence of God's
Gracious forgiveness and love.

Open our heart to enthrone the anointing,
We need to be willing; to enjoy being a vessel of God.
When angered – Ignore the ignorance of others.
Pick up the pieces and move on.
Let God show you how to build your ark and
You are saved. Pray every day. Noah did!

Step 5

Admitted to God, to ourselves,
and to other human beings
The exact nature of our wrongs

Eyes Wide-Shut

All you are-we need to know.
For, God wants us to be your bro…
Help us find the balance beam,
To carry you across the stream
Out to the desert, dry and calm
To find Gods' self-reliant arm..

FOOL'S GOLD

The camper sits on wealthy sand
The trover waves his wand,
And, in a pilfered ecstasy
The ocean is a pond.

With clarity the depth of which,
By some has gone unnoticed
And yet the depth is clearly marked,
The bottom is not bogus.

The noisy sand in symphony
Now calls out to its' prober
"I have the wealth, of which you seek
And I am not an ogre."

"Neath weed and reed
Of well-aged seed
Of lagers' brew and yoga
A king in pride
It streaks the tide
In altogether toga."

The hunter digs his toes in deep
And waves his little basket
To find the wealth,
of which he seeks
When, he just has to ask it.

Again the sand in reasoned rhyme
Riddles to the seeker
"I am the prize for which you queer
Queried now and meeker."
"Gods" own light has shown me here
Though fools may tend to wander
I'm humble perfect in my place
But, you still drive a Honda.

My simple grain is Cadillac.
A prize, the beach so grand
I have achieved my destiny.
In service to God's land.

Step 6

*We are entirely ready to have God
remove all these defects of character*

Rebellion is Fatal

Floating in the sea of alcohol,
God chose to show me ground.
I took a step; then four or five
Now, six is where I'm bound.
The tool I have is fashioned prayer
And honest conversation.
With God on board-
I know I'm headed for salvation.
No timely debates needed
Nor, filibuster stand.
My H.P. beckons me to walk
the footprints in the sand.
He has for me some sandals,
Or even horse to ride.
He will even carry me,
If I am by His side.

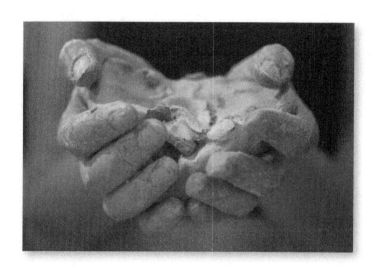

Step 7

*Humbly asked Him
to remove our short comings*

LORD I AM NOT WORTHY

Oh Lord, though I may fumble,
please, help keep me humble.
Take from me the foul of face,
which puts me into loss of grace.
To follow your will,
even though I stumble.

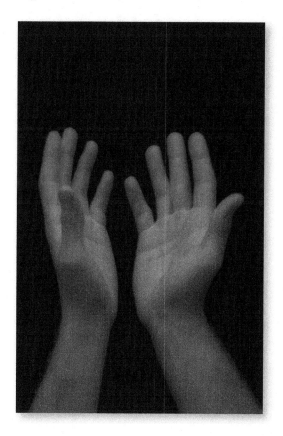

Step 8

Made a list of all persons we had harmed, and became willing to make amends to them all.

A QUIET OBJECTIVE VIEW

The grass is green,
But, under the foot

Ants build motels
And grubs eat the root.

Bedeviled, sick emotions ride.
As fear conspires with our pride,

To hide
Our bad behavior, deep inside

As sick as our secrets are,
We sweep clean under the rug of wrath

Cleaning our side,
To walk a newly made path

To forgive, let go and prosper.
Who did we hurt or wound the senses.

A sponsors guide is recommended,
To avoid the pitfalls of our defenses.

Let down your guard,
And ride the wake

Commune with nature,
For your own sake.

Prayer of True Repentance

Dear God,

Dry up our tears of remorse, which lead us to death like Judas and Esau.

In your goodness and kindness please help and bless us with the true gift of repentance.

Circumscribe in our hearts the value of your love and mercy.

Save us.

Step 9

Made direct amends to such people wherever possible, except when to do so would injure them or others

SERENITY

God, grant me the serenity
To accept the things
I cannot change

Courage to change the
Things I can, and the
Wisdom to know the difference

By: Reinhold Niebuhr

Step 10

Continued to take personal inventory and when we were wrong promptly admitted it.

Patience and Persistence

Persistently working to alleviate the emotional hangover of negative feelings, we gambit to a rebirth.

Admitting and correcting our mistakes, we encounter our own self-worth.

Patiently using weapons of self-restraint and honest analysis, like a new dawn of sunshine we blossom with restraint of tongue and pen.

Banishing the darkness of silent scorn and sulking, we cap the necessity to make amends.

Step 11

Sought through prayer and
meditation to improve
our conscious contact with God
as we understood Him,
praying only for the knowledge of His will and
the power to carry that out.

WAITING FOR THE SNOW TO FALL

As I steal away for quiet, in my head, there is a riot,
over many a respectful rule and forgotten etiquette.
While thinking, nearly rabid, "Why yes indeed,"
there is a habit.
"Respect the Lord on the Sabbath."

While the world is covered in sickness, hatred, ill-will and
famine,
the creation, as it was conceived, is still pristine.
A simple snowflake dances on gusts of polarized air,
and then is carried back up to its' lofty chair.
Finally, with each twist and turn, it lands on spot of Gods'
concern.

Traveling through the underbrush of my mind.
I encounter my God of a loving kind.
He is justice and patience and He is sublime.
As quiet dances, it does not stomp.
It is not circumstance and pomp.
Knowledge and power of His will-understanding is a beast
that levels off
within us each.

IF I KNEW THEN?

Once we see
where we were then,
It's too late
to go back again.

If we could
We'd only find,
What lingers most
The thoughts of mind.

We'd think we could,
change all that was.
But, thinking is
that's all it does.

For what is now,
has come to be.
From what was then,
once we can see.

For as it were,
it had to be.
More oft' than not,
we ne'er can see.

More than today,
are only dreams.
We see today,
as if it seems.

That as we thought,
it ne'er would be.
Did come upon,
too soon for me.

Step 12

Having had a spiritual awakening
as a result of these steps,
We tried to carry this message to alcoholics,
and to practice these principles
In all our affairs

AS WINTER WANES

Beyond the barren branches
Cotton covered clouds
The sequin squinted sky
Shadows spider-webbed silhouettes

Chipped chimney curls
Winding without way
As twigs twitch tauntingly
Behind black billows

Over the trunks twisted torso
Of birds nest brown
The whittled, white, wooden windows
Visit virgin vacillations

Half-here, half-haunted
Sleeping beauty slumbers
The kingly kiss kindling
Warm weather wonders

SOUL FOOD

We bring the food and then we wonder,
If and when, the will have hunger.
"A tisket, a tasket, a little big book basket."
I know my friend is on the cusp.
In Gods' time, he will come to sup,
Or, he will line an early casket.

Do not bight the hand that feeds,
But shake it 'til it plants the seed.
Of hole in soul and broken spirit.
The tree of life we'll climb and grow.
He'll be with you head to toe.
Stay around and you will hear it.
With each step, a little story,
About the alcohol beast- so gory!

Do not worry, no more sorry.

Hurry! Hurry! Step right up
And fill your cup.

Left., right, left, right—march to glory!

THE OCEAN LINER

The ocean breeze blew burrowing some lines upon my face.
My eyes were focused o'er the waves; horizon in its' place.

The glimmer of the water was sparkling from the sun-
Azure in its' color. White sails blew one by one.

The mini-mounds were ample but, mallow marsh was most.
And, as the seagulls sailed, they underlined the coast.

The surfers in their skivvies were shark fins in disguise.
And, as the curls approached they utilized the rise.

The foamy crests then landed On seaweed piled mounds
A couple jaunting in the sand was leashed –up to their
hounds

I wondered why the jet ski? Its' speed was so dis-pace.
The palms were dancing lazily. The day was not a race.

And then, some winded surfer plodded through the sand.
The hot dog bought a hot dog at the hot dog stand.

A biker walked the concrete path; with racer at his side.
He dropped some garbage in the can, Pollution he defied.

And then, some little campers with boogie boards in tow
Descended o'er the mushy mounds, to water- good to go.

A lady and her lover were walking hand in hand.
They smiled at each other. For them, the day was planned.

A volley ball came into play. The server was so steady;
But, with the wind, a jaunty gust. The other team-not ready.

A four-pack family soon approached. One babe upon moms' hip
With pail and shovel –daughter two built castles in the dip.

Now, kites of green and orange hovered like a flock.
The tails of each electrified Like eels of neon stock

The lifeguard in his tower, to save he did intend.
He spent the day in baneful watch; but, he did not descend.

THE FISHERS ON THE BREAK

(Harmony and Passion)
Dana Point, California

Some came to sleep,
Some came to fish,
While scoters surfed the caps.

And some to dive
And some to soar
With relatives perhaps!

They parasailed
The pools they flailed
While skaters screeched the call.

Whose sky to race
Whose passion paced
With short among the tall.

They walked the sand
They walked the marsh
While sanderlings did scurry

For some to float
And some to perch
All with determined flurry!

THE PHOENIX

(September 11, 2011)

It was a day like all the others,
For the sons who left their mothers.
The towers of fame,
Went down in flame.
From ashes arose the daughters' grave.
Firefighters-too late to save.
And, out among the screeching mob,
Fathers; hearts began to sob.
Of aunts and uncles, friends and foes,
Ten years of tribulation and woes.
The lights now shine on every star,
Up in heaven- way off far.

The Greatest Commandment

Love the Lord, your God, with all your being and your neighbor as yourself. This implies that you must love yourself as God loves you.

God's love is a willingness to love and be loved. It is infinite and divine. It can only be achieved through His grace.

> The price I pay
> Is to pray, pray, pray
> To Him, from me, for you.
> To keep it – I must give it away.

The Lord wants a personal relationship with me, you and all of His children. He is a caring father who wants only the best for His offspring. He has promised us blessings through his covenant with Noah and God is truth and cannot lie or deceive.

THE FLOWER AND
THE BREEZE

(Suddenly,) I was in a field of purple mountain laurel,-
(An enigma in itself).
When a gentle breeze forced each delicate stem to lean;
As if- in search of a better view.

And as they tossed back their heads,
playing peek-a-boo with the sun,
I admired the determination of a bumble
bee, as it darted, to alight –its'
Desired bulls-eye.

Enveloped in this breath taking
panorama; I was inebriated by the
passionate aroma.

I curtsied to the warmth of the golden
sun-bowing as each flower had
done. I was a mountain laurel turning to face the wind.

Transformed, I could feel strength in the
calmness of its' serenity and as it surrounded
me I was enraptured by its' touch.

DENISE

Denise, my little angel
you have come back to me.
Fly no more as stranger
but, rest in wing-ed tree.

Your face will bloom a smile.
Your eyes will simply rest.
Away from good and evil,
the tree of life to test

The thunder of the cymbals,
will hum a lullaby.
And a clap of lightening,
will twinkle in your eye.

10 Year Testimony Of Sobriety And In Praise Of A Sponsor

I drank myself to sleep as usual and shortly wound up in another Detox. I had been to "AA meetings" at Rehab and other detoxes but I didn't get it. But this time "God gave me a gift", I not only listened, I heard. It was our own Deana, my sponsor, who carried the message and spoke at this meeting. I will be forever grateful. I can't tell you what she said. I was too screwed up to remember. But, whatever it was, it was what I needed to hear. And, whenever I speak, I always pray that someone hears what they need to hear. If the AA message reaches just one Alcoholic, I have carried it well.

That was my last Detox. I knew I had to jump into AA 200% with both feet even if it was to prove that it didn't work!

But, today I'm living life to the fullest; Proof that it does work if you follow the path thoroughly. All these celebrants are proof it works.

Surrender and Triumph, What a concept!!

It's a good thing I'm Polish and a dumb blond- It made perfect sense to me!

Seriously, this disease is a killer; a destroyer of families and a thief that robs you from yourself. It takes your happiness and your kindness and your faith.

If you're new, keep coming. One year Anniversaries are the most special and follow suggestions.

Lynn's Unfinished Autobiography

"It's a girl!"

The nurse was ecstatic in her announcement of a healthy child born to Ruth and Eugene in Jan. 1949.

The parents had previously had three still births and one boy with heart problems who only lived four hours. Little Lynn Marie was not only the apple of her parents eyes but the whole cornucopia.

Her 10 year older step-brother was hoping for a boy but, as soon as he saw her, he fell in love. She delighted the entire family with her giggles and coos and having inherited her mom's superior intelligence was a whiz in school and solving brain teasers to the amazement of her parents' friends.

She was born and raised in Queens, NY. She remembers playing with all the neighborhood kids. She has a very competitive nature.

At six years of age her father's death not only claimed his life but also her brother's childhood.

Necessity dictated that he start working to help enhance the family income. A $10,000 death benefit for a cop didn't go very far.

She remembers sitting in the basket of her brother's bike as he traced the circumference of the circle created by the streetlights. She basked in the kindness of his attention which she earnestly desired.

It was the best of times. It was the worst of times. I was a kid. What the H-E- double hockey sticks did I know anyway? And, yet, from early on; my existence was ruled by acceptance and the courage to change that which I could. This, I came to believe is the key to a serene yet exuberantly fulfilling existence.

I thought of hiding the evidence, but, it would never work. I just didn't like the idea of being a disappointment to mom. So, taking a deep breath, I opened the front door, and like the lit fuse on a powder keg blazed through the house and into the kitchen.

"I'm sorry mom, but I hate the dam things. I forgot they were in my pocket I had thrown my jacket in the pile with everyone else's. When the basketball landed, I heard the crunch."

Moms' powder blue eyes scrunched shut momentarily. The skin on her Santa Claus cheeks stretched tightly as she pensively pondered how to juggle the bills to pay for the repairs. This was her main concern. Mom understood thirteen. It was tough for a girl to compete athletically and still look 'cool' with glasses on. In the early '60's, glasses did not make a fashion statement. They only emphasized a physical impairment. And boys, they could be so cruel at that age. Well, maybe, cruel is a bad choice of words—more like, -thoughtless and unrelenting in their merciless taunts, which they believed to be so humorous.

Humorous, ha! Now, that's a laugh! Even my bean-pole of a brother thought he was being funny when he called me, "four eyes". Stab me in the back and pull it out through my heart, why don't you? Four eyes, -why don't you just call me –"Mrs. Potato Head" – and stick big yellow, oversized shoes on my feet to shuffle around in. Honestly! How dare he?

I, however, with the sight of a leopard, (I could spot anything) newly fixed glasses perched upon the bridge of my cute, acute proboscis, rode the waves to shore.

The courage to change that which I can-became a babysitting job at the age of thirteen; and, coupled with the genetic ability to be frugal, I acquired contact lenses.

Sighted shores unseen, I traveled new horizons.

And, while time is inevitable; and, we cannot delay its passing, nor, change its outcome; a fragment of time does exist between the thought and the written word.

Know That I Love You

Know that I love you
For all that I am worth
You have helped me to believe in.

Know that I love you
For you have lifted me to a plateau; but,
you did not leave me there-you have come to join me.

And, you have seen me-without my beauty
and, I have strutted like a peacock.
So, know that I love you.

When I have spoken foolish thoughts,
you did not laugh;
but, shared your foolish thoughts with me.

Know that I love you.
For you have seen my tears,
and, did not prey upon my fears.

You have watched them flow;
but, did not interrupt their path.
Heavy upon your ears-at times- stinging like ice pellets.

But, you did not take shelter.
You walked in the rain.
Know that I love you.

From Here To Eternity

May the windows of the world be open,
as the angel-drawn caravan arrives.
The trumpets of gold gleaming,
the glow of dawn streaming.
As each white-winged soul wanders by
shrouded in silks and satins.
Silent and serene
As they approach the end
of their timeless journey.

Lynn with Her Son Jay

Printed in the United States
By Bookmasters